1

2

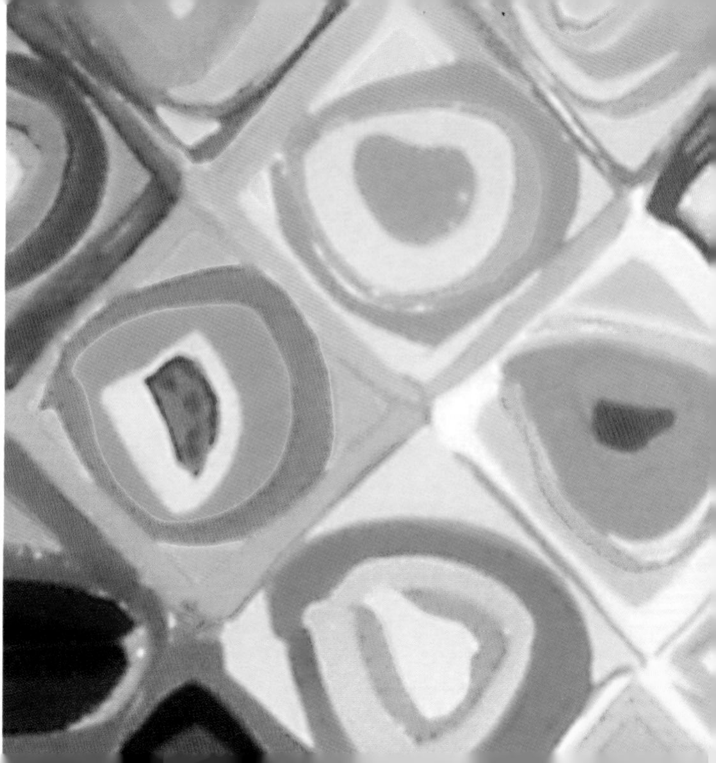

4

5

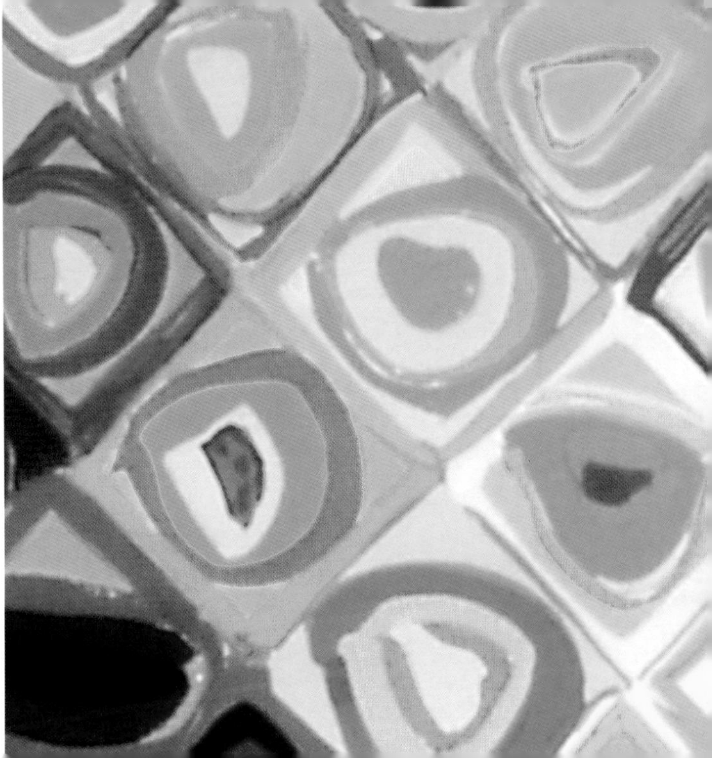

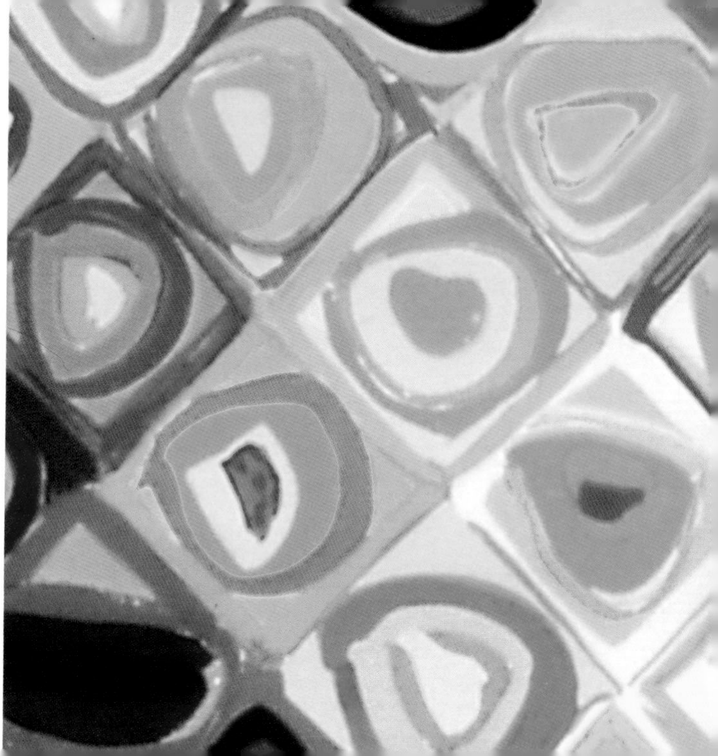

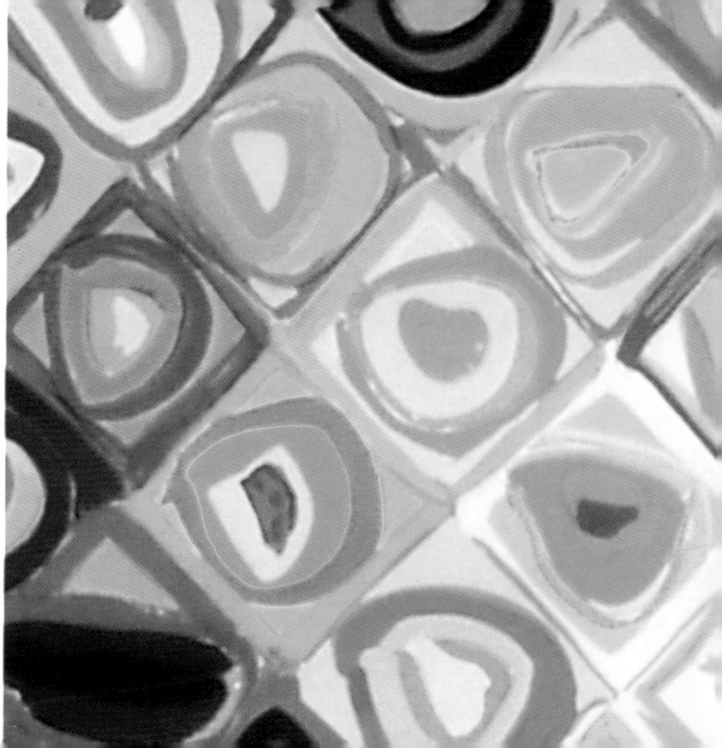

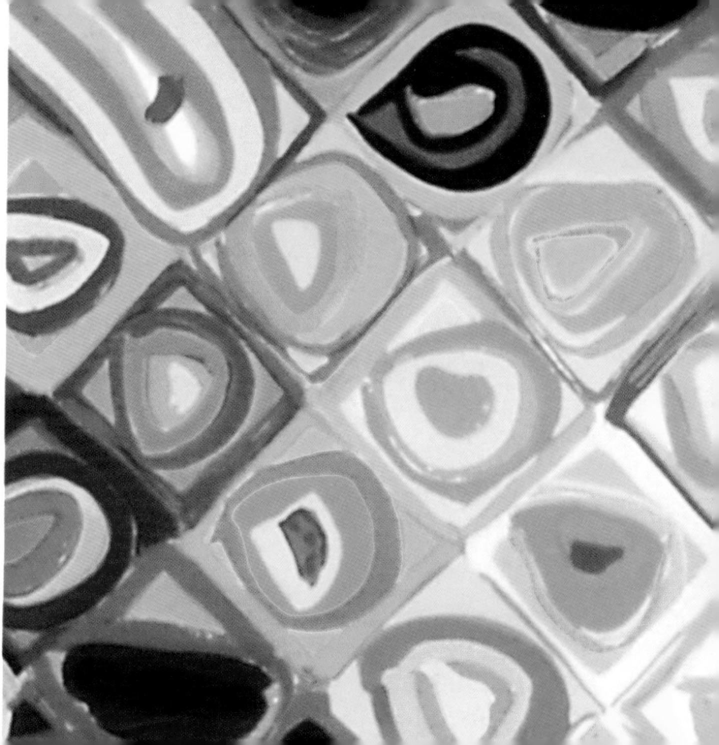

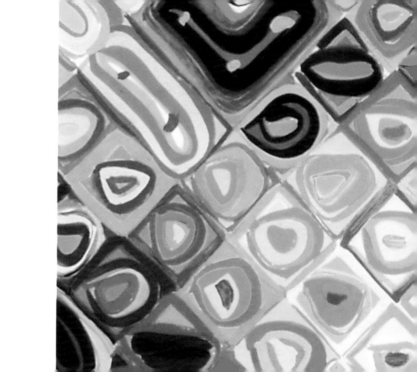

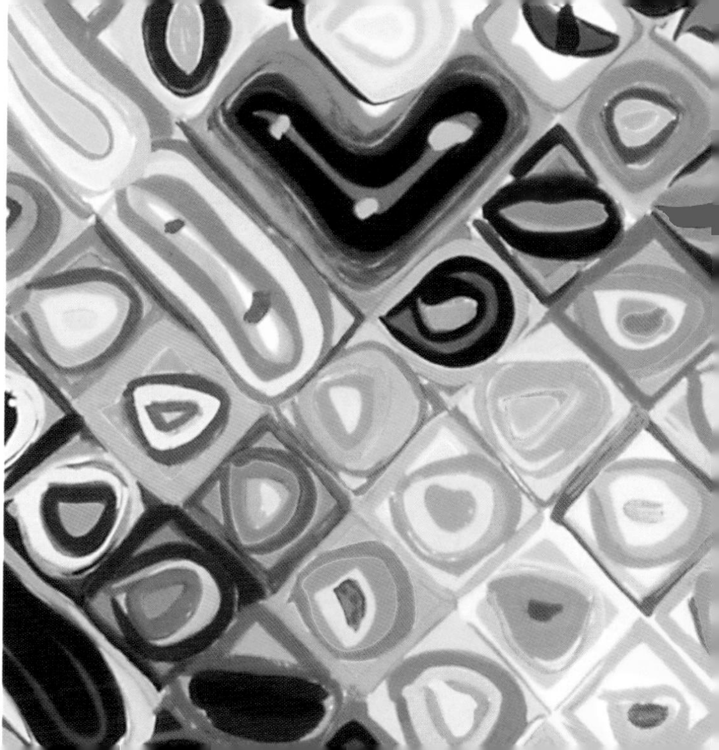

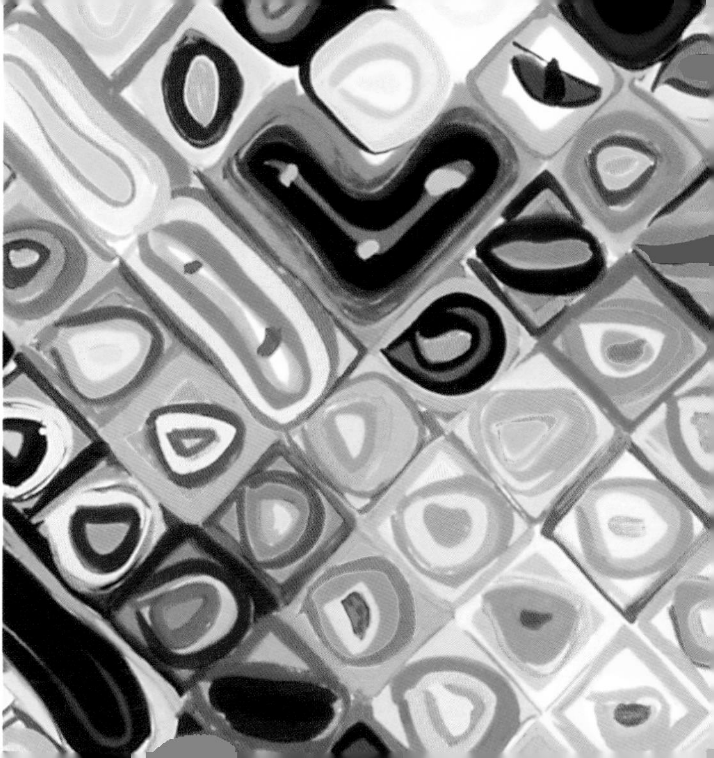

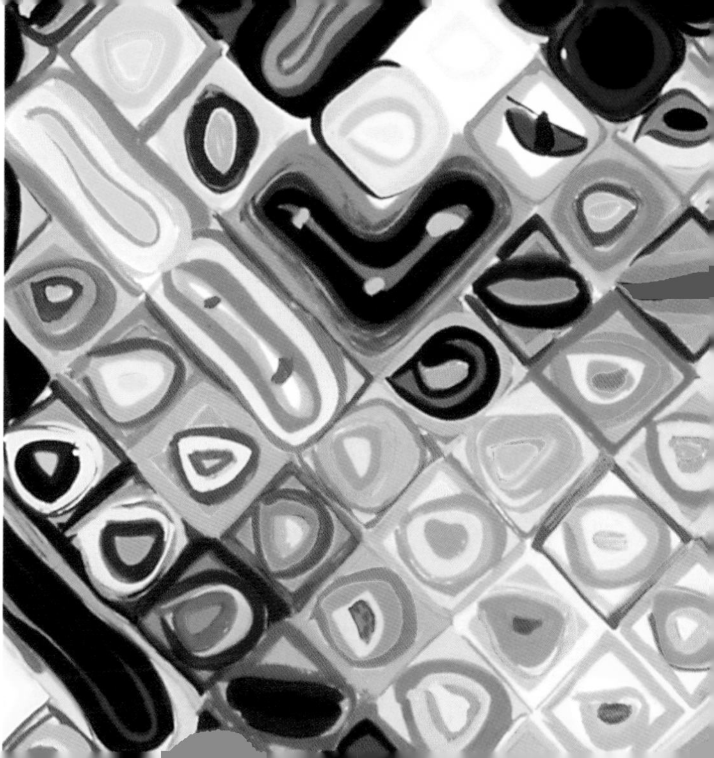

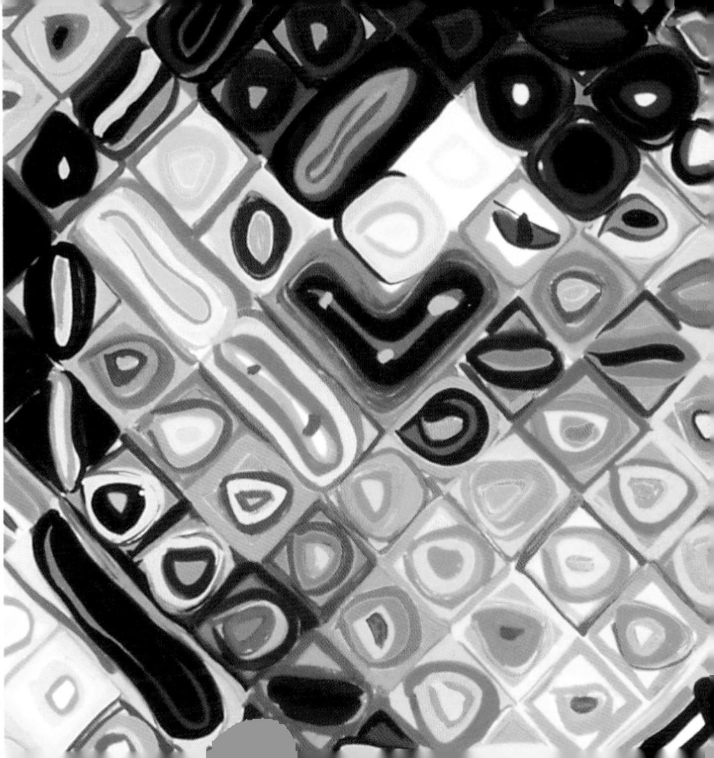

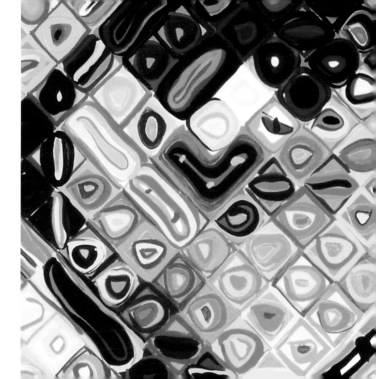

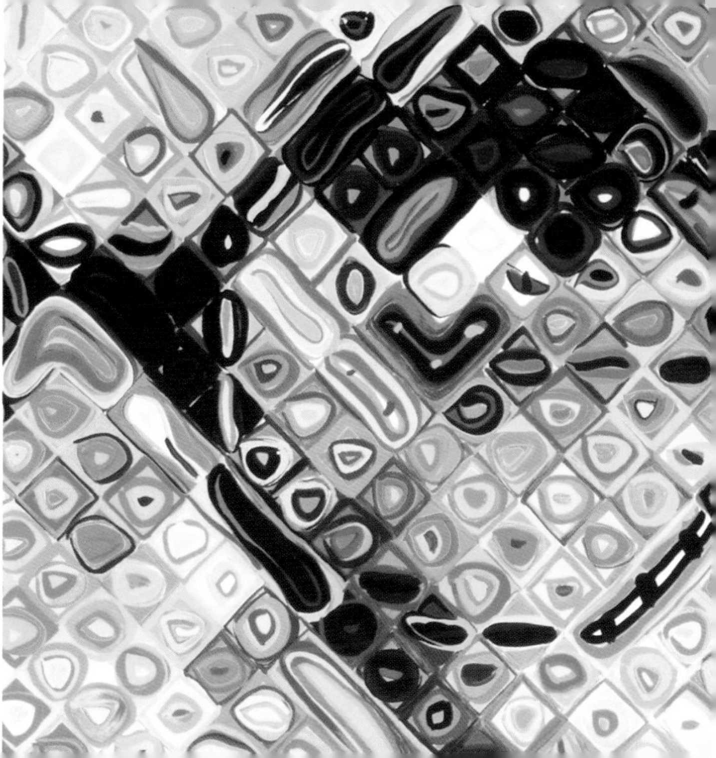

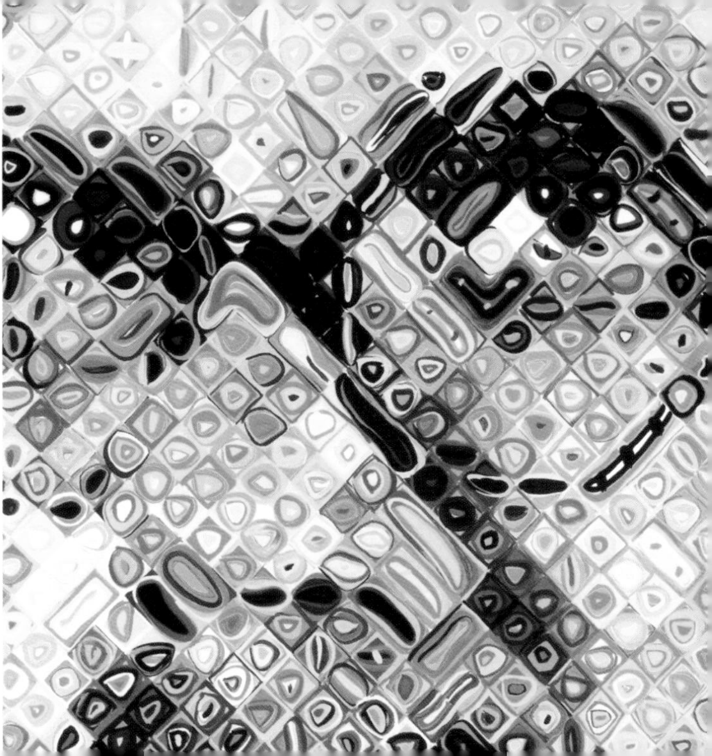

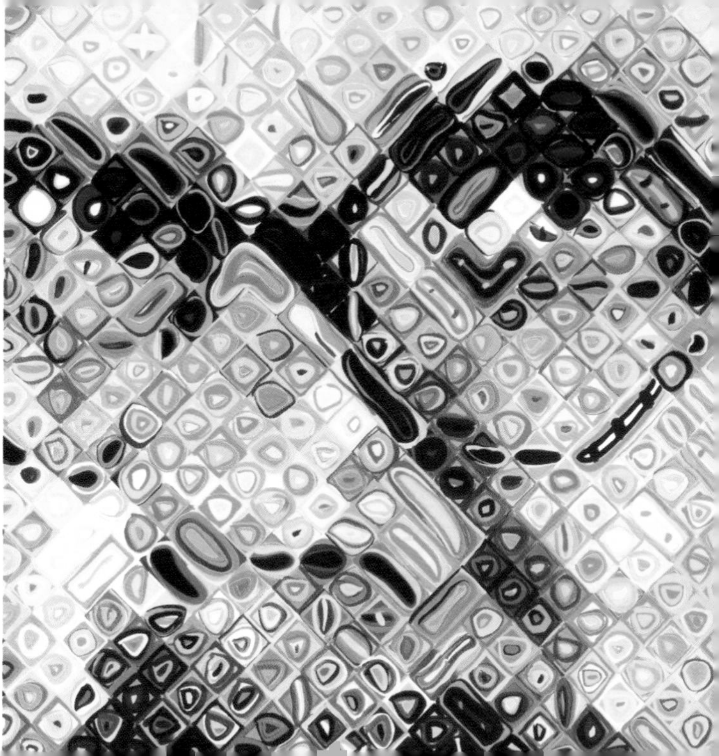

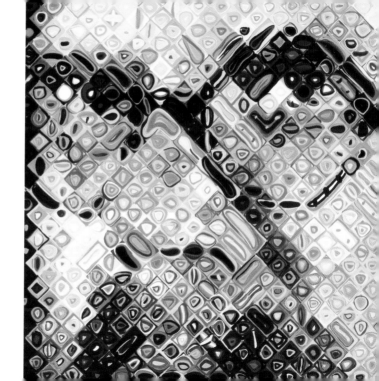

8

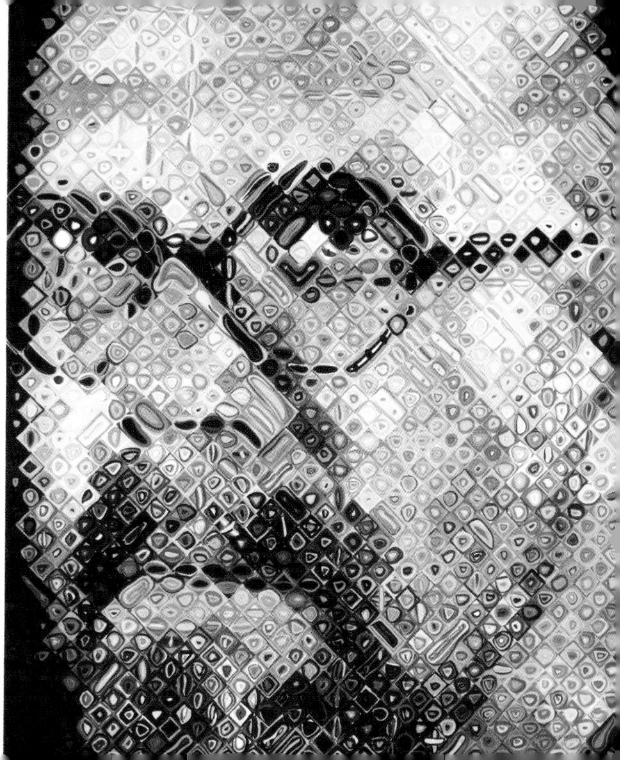

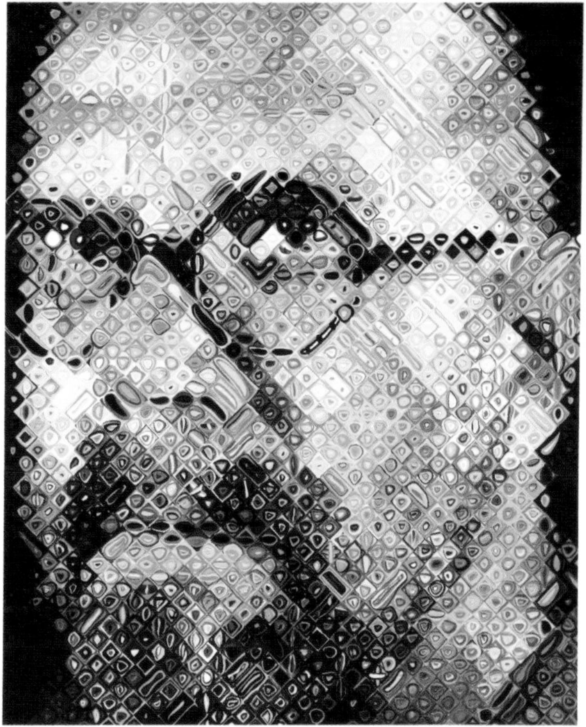

For nearly four decades, Chuck Close has worked from photographs, making striking portraits of his family, friends, and fellow artists. More than any other subject, however, he has painted himself. The first such self-portrait, begun in 1967, has been followed by nearly 100 more in a range of media, including paintings, drawings, photographs, and prints. Unified by the consistent image of the artist's face, this body of work invites us to see the expansive possibilities hidden in a familiar image.

This flipbook is being published on the occasion of the exhibition *Chuck Close: Self-Portraits 1967–2005*, organized jointly by the San Francisco Museum of Modern Art and the Walker Art Center, Minneapolis.

CHUCK CLOSE
Self-Portrait 2000 (detail)
111-color screenprint; edition of 80
65 1/2 x 54 1/8 inches
Collection Walker Art Center, Minneapolis
Gift of the artist

Screenprint printed at Brand X, New York
Screenprint published by Pace Editions, Inc., New York
Courtesy the artist and Pace Editions, Inc.